MW01265350

LESSON PLANS
for LIFE

GARY MILLEN

Lesson Plans for Life
Copyright © 2021 by Gary Millen

Tellwell Talent
www.tellwell.ca

ISBN
978-0-2288-4831-8 (Hardcover)
978-0-2288-4830-1 (Paperback)
978-0-2288-4832-5 (eBook)

CONTENTS

ACKNOWLEDGMENTS

I would like to thank the following people for their assistance with this book:

My wife, Linda, for her guidance in every step from start to finish.

My daughter, Audra, and my son, Vincent, for not only encouraging me to undertake this project but also providing some of the content.

Alfreida Degroot for typing the entire manuscript and for her kind support.

INTRODUCTION

My purpose in writing this book is to pass along the scores of strategies and techniques that I have found successful in my fifty plus years working with students, parents, teachers and school administrators.

During my career and beyond, I have served as a teacher, principal, administrator, mathematics consultant and mentor to young boys. My revelations will go beyond mathematics instruction to how I was often able to empower my clients with many other valuable life skills. My experiences have allowed me to become more and more aware that the scope of our teaching is quite deficient. When I see so many of our citizens, young and old, making bad choices regarding their health, safety and financial independence, choices that negatively impact them for years going forward, I'm convinced we could, and should, be doing so much more. That includes education that goes beyond traditional academic expectations but could be every bit as important.

Though I will reveal a sampling of the mathematical lessons I'm proud to share, I intend for this book to be filled, chapter by chapter, with the stories I hope will help the reader use what I have learned and developed to create a brighter future for all.

PROLOGUE

*You see things and you say, why? But I dream
things that never were, and I say, why not?*
—George Bernard Shaw

F or the past fifty plus years, my wife Linda and I have been blessed with the opportunity to be involved in the education of young students. Over these years, we have watched young people grow and develop into successful adults. But at the same time, we have also witnessed scores fall far short of their potential to become productive citizens. It pains us to see young athletes, for example, who can do wonders with their powers on the court or on the field, only to go rapidly downhill when the cheering stops.

Sadly, despite the hard work of thousands of very dedicated teachers, we are still selling our children short by not instilling critical life skills and the strategies and motivation needed for success beyond graduation. John, a personable young Black student, had a full two-year athletic scholarship to a small liberal arts junior college in the Midwest. However, he wasn't prepared for a lifestyle much different from the comfort of the "hood" and lasted but two short weeks in college. Back in the inner city, he saw some of his high school friends driving nice cars and buying nice clothes with their income from dealing drugs. Needless to say, it was not long before John was selling drugs, too. This venture ended tragically with his arrest. John spent the next nine years in the penitentiary.

As far back as I can remember, the dropout phenomenon has been a problem that has never been successfully addressed. When these individuals, many from poor families, transition through our school systems, they are sooner or later faced with the realization of how ill-prepared they are for the demands of high school or the opportunities that lie beyond. After all, which of us would like to go to work each day only to be reminded of our failures? Therefore, these young students are tempted to find fulfillment in negative endeavors.

Be assured, on most any day, there exist several frustrated and angry young men walking the streets of our cities with the potential to make decisions that will lead to disaster for them and their victims.

There is so much more we could be doing to empower tomorrow's citizens with appropriate life skills. In the chapters that follow, I will focus on how positivity and proactivity worked for me and the many teachers, parents and school personnel I had the pleasure of working with. I will address the topics of safety, math, family relationships, values, money matters, tutoring, mentoring, grading and classroom management, with an emphasis on my love of teaching math. I will include a sampling of the lessons I developed that I found very effective. And I hope to pass along many good examples and stories that I hope will touch the hearts and souls of my readers.

> *The best argument in the world won't*
> *change a single person's mind. The only*
> *thing that will do that is a good story.*
> —Richard Powers, novelist

MY BEGINNINGS

Good Friday, April 3, 1942, was a "good Friday" for me because it was the day of my birth. My earliest remembrance is as a three-year-old. My father had just lost his job, and I overheard my parents discussing what they were going to do. I asked my mother if we were going to die. She assured me we were going to be okay.

I grew up the youngest of four boys, and I had two sisters, one older, one younger. We lived in a big old farmhouse on a bluff overlooking the Mississippi River. My siblings and I attended a small, two-room country school located about two miles from our home. My younger sister had only one boy in her class.

As a six-year-old, I tried to talk my mother out of sending me to school since I could not read anyway. She told me not to worry. They would teach me to read. Each day, we would walk to school, often stopping along the way to join others. If we walked through the woods, our trek was about a mile and a half. Two of my older brothers were recruited to serve as school custodians which required our early arrival, especially in the colder months, to stoke the furnace. That way, by the time the teachers and other students arrived the building was fairly warm.

In the third grade, I was honored to be appointed the downstairs custodian where the classes for grades one to four were held. My responsibilities required sweeping floors each evening, after sprinkling them with red sweeping compound. In the morning, I would fill the water jugs at the outdoor water pump for everyone to drink throughout the school day. I also patted the chalk erasers so they would be ready for use the next school day. We spent lots of time using the chalkboards for lessons and drills. My pay at the end of each month was one dollar. I was always proud to use my money to buy a few groceries for the family. However, I remember the one month when I was rewarded with a seashell collection instead of any money. I still have my seashells, some seventy years later.

I believe it was in third grade that I developed my first taste for teaching. I got into a debate with my classmates over which was greater, one-fourth or one-third. My classmates felt one-fourth was larger than one-third because four is larger than three. To make matters worse, Miss Scroggins, our teacher, was leaning their way. I remember drawing two rectangles, dividing one into four parts and other into three parts. Upon shading one-fourth of one and one-third of the other, I enlightened the teacher and my classmates. Sixty plus years later, I am still drawing pictures for my math students.

I believe my humble beginnings had a lot to do with my desire to help others. My parents both came from large families and were raised in a farming culture. I never knew my grandparents, as they were deceased prior to my birth. My father was somewhat of a garden farmer. I was never fond of the hot summer days when I was expected to weed and hoe vegetables. We realized a small income selling sweet corn, tomatoes, potatoes and strawberries up and down the highway. We gave most of our crops away to family and friends.

Another way we supplemented our income was by harvesting wild blackberries in the massive woods behind our house. Our mother would fill a few mason jars with ice water and seal the lids with wax paper. Each of us, mother, brother, sister and I, would place our water jars in a bucket and hike far into the woods where the good picking awaited. Our mother was the best berry picker, as she knew how to trample down the sticker bushes to get where the best and largest berries were hiding. I remember many times carrying a water bucket of luscious berries in each hand as we returned from the woods. Our harvest was usually sold to the pie company in the nearby town of East Moline. On a good day, we would realize enough profit to buy groceries for the whole week.

Even though we came from a large family, I recall often feeling lonely. My older brothers spent their summer months farming on my oldest sister and brother-in-law's large farm. Most of my school friends lived a good distance away from our house. We had no air-conditioning, but after a few years we moved into the basement, which stayed somewhat cooler on the hot days of summer. We also had no indoor plumbing, so we had to draw water for drinking, cooking and bathing from the well in the front of our house. I am not sure if the lack of sanitation from the open well may have contributed to some of my ailments, but I remember suffering from many bouts of the stomach flu in my youth.

The winters also presented some painful memories, as we used an outhouse for our toilet needs. We young ones did avail ourselves of a "thunder mug," a small tin bucket that we kept under our beds. On the coldest of winter days, I would dress for school behind the basement furnace where it was fairly warm. It was a blessing when we were able to afford a coal stoker, which would feed the furnace throughout the night. My job was to fill the hopper with coke (coal particles) from the coal bin. We took our weekly baths in a round, galvanized tub partially filled with water. Our mother would heat a tea kettle of water to warm our bath.

Our mother was an extremely hard worker. When she wasn't in our garden, she was cleaning house, sewing clothes, doctoring and preparing all our meals. To make matters worse, our father was always inviting friends for dinner. I never went to a barber until I was a junior in high school because my mother also served as the family barber. Not only did she give us all our haircuts, but she also cut hair for many of my father's friends (free of charge). She was so happy when she could afford electric clippers that replaced the scissors she had squeezed for so long.

My father suffered from several childhood diseases and seldom held a steady job. When he graduated from high school, my brother Jack found a steady job with a local corporation to help with finances. Every Friday, upon payday, he would stop at a local market and purchase five pounds of ground beef for us to live on during the week.

One of my father's many jobs was driving a big rack truck for a nearby mental institution. At that time, male mental patients were required to work the fields caring for the farm crops. Dad's job was to transport the patients from one field to another. Sometimes, he would have fifteen to twenty men standing in the back of his truck. Dad was very kind to his charges, but many of the bosses were not. On one occasion, I overheard one of the big shots laughing about how he would punish the Blacks. (He actually used the N-word).

I remember one occasion when a hospital employee stopped by our home accompanied by a mental patient he was overseeing. Times like these offered me the opportunity to chat with the patients. They were eager for someone to talk with. One patient, named Andy, told me how famous he was and that when he died, he was going to be buried at Arlington National Cemetery. Quickly, his supervisor intervened in our conversation saying, "You're going to be buried in the hospital cemetery with all the other nuts!"

My first driving experience was a small Allis Chalmers tractor, which I had to crank to get started. I would plow small gardens for families up and down the highway. I never asked for pay and sometimes did not receive any. On one occasion, I used my tractor to pull a motorist out of the ditch and refused to accept any pay. The father of one of my friends who lived across the highway witnessed this ordeal and fiercely scolded me for not accepting any money. I did enjoy helping people, but I could have used the money to help my family.

In 1957, my brother Jack was drafted into the Army and our mother found it necessary to find work. She accepted a position as a nurse's aide at Moline Public Hospital. Soon after that, our dad went to work at Riverside Foundry in Bettendorf, Iowa. Prior to my eighth-grade year, my small school district consolidated with East Moline Public Schools. In one year, I went from a class of five boys to a freshman class of over 400 students. Needless to say, the five of us were social misfits but academically did quite well!

My sophomore year in high school, I gave up playing a winter sport so I could assume the job of having my own paper route. I now had my first steady income. My senior year, I gave up my route and took a job working at an uncle's farm earning a dollar an hour. In the summer months, he would let me work up to twelve hours a day. That provided me twelve dollars in one day for hoeing dwarf apple trees and loading bales of hay. My uncle tried to talk me out of college by offering me somewhat of a partnership in his highly lucrative apple farming business. I can still hear him saying, "Why would you want to be a schoolteacher when you could be a successful farmer with me?" However, I was now eighteen years old and had experienced the satisfaction that comes with helping others with their studies. I saw teaching as my path to a meaningful career.

Upon graduation from United Township High School, I enrolled at Moline Community College, which is now Blackhawk Junior College. I enrolled in a full load of courses each day and found a second shift job at Riverside Foundry in Bettendorf, Iowa. Between classes and work, I would sometimes sneak a quick nap on the hard benches in the PE locker room. Then, many hours later, upon returning home from work, I would find myself finishing my homework around midnight in preparation for my morning classes. In two years, I had saved enough money to pay for my junior and senior years at Illinois State University. In addition, I was financially able to send money home to my dad to pay for a prosthesis, which he needed due to losing his leg to diabetes.

Upon graduating in the spring of 1964, I was offered my first teaching position in the inner city of Peoria, Illinois. I was interviewed over the phone, and I was promised that my $500 student loan would be forgiven if I taught in the inner-city school where I had done my student teaching. The salary for my first year was $7,800!

The principal at Roosevelt Junior High School was a Navy veteran who was known to run a "tight ship". Every classroom had a wooden paddle hanging by the entry door. Teachers were expected to use the paddle when necessary to maintain discipline. Any student whose behavior was inappropriate was sent to the principal's office for an automatic swat. Legend has it that once a young lad received a swat before the principal realized he had just come into the office hoping to enroll in the school.

In 1969, I was recruited to teach mathematics and coach sports for Peoria Public Schools' gifted program. Students were selected for Washington Gifted School based on teacher recommendations and high scores on a battery of aptitude and achievement tests. I was now in a program where discipline was hardly an issue. I taught at the gifted school for nineteen years. A lot was expected of teachers at Washington Gifted School. We were required to attend workshops in instructional techniques taught by the best educators across the state and nationally. Eventually, we were required to make presentations of our own.

In 1989, I began teaching and coaching at Woodruff High School. Two years later, I moved to administration coordinating Peoria Public Schools' math program. I had taken many teams to state Mathcounts competitions while teaching at Washington School. As math coordinator, I implemented a district Mathcounts program for all Peoria Public Schools eighth grade teachers. I saw to it that they were even paid an additional salary increment.

In 1994, I became principal of Calvin Coolidge Middle School where I was able to implement many of my dreams. In 2001, after seven years as a principal, I retired from Peoria Public Schools. However, my leisure days did not last long, as I was enticed by many area principals and superintendents to return as a math consultant. For the next several years, I mentored math teachers, developed units and did model teaching. I also completed training at the Children's Home as a respite worker. I was assigned young boys from dysfunctional families to mentor. I am still involved with several of these families today.

I will attempt to share my successes and failures in the chapters that follow in the hope that I can pass on to those who work with our youth the many strategies and programs that worked for our school.

—Education is the most powerful weapon which you can use to change the world.
Nelson Mandela

Students at Sycamore School

The photo above of the first through fourth grade students at Sycamore Grade School was taken in 1950. Sycamore Grade School was located near the small town of Rapid City, Illinois. The author can be found in the third row from the front proudly displaying a silver badge on his bib overalls. Several of his girlfriends can also be found in the picture.

LIFE SKILLS

recently purchased a book online titled *Life Skills*, a book I had half seriously thought of writing myself. I have been blessed to have the mentoring and guidance of so many who have gone ahead of me and who have gifted me with valuable life skills. Now, I want to see this wisdom and knowledge passed on by using our school personnel, churches, sports programs and community organizations to create an environment that fosters mentoring.

There is a saying that goes, "Learn from the mistakes of others because you can't live long enough to make them all yourself." That quote resonates with me because I am disheartened to see so many young people today making bad choices and having to learn the hard way. Too often, these choices will impact them negatively for years to come.

Several years ago, Peoria Public Schools put an emphasis on several life skills with a middle school program titled, "Consumer Education." Students were exposed to simple hand tools and instructed in basic home maintenance skills. Some emphasis was on preventative maintenance, such as changing filters and electrical repairs. Students also received financial advice, were taught to write checks and to reconcile their bank accounts. My students enjoyed these classes, which were a good start, but obviously the learning needed to go much farther, both then and now.

Classes or courses in life skills could well be done remotely where instruction could be enhanced by experts in various fields and shared across an entire school district. Many homework assignments would consist of students consulting with an older adult, parent or relative about how they would go about handling a problem or situation that the student was likely to experience in the future. Their grades could be determined by their consistency in reporting their findings. What great value would come from healthy family discussions around the evening dinner. As an example, in teaching a unit on values, a typical assignment might require students to interview an adult about why integrity is important and then share their revelations with their teachers and classmates.

MONEY

ar too often, I have witnessed people struggle financially for reasons that could have been avoided with some simple tips or guidance. Most recently, many of us are bombarded with Internet or telephone scams that are so enticing that many victims, both young and old, are taken in. It hurts to see friends paying for services they do not need and often will never use. This is just one way people begin to rack up unnecessary debt, often without a clear picture of how it will add up in the long run.

Recently, a friend and I were attempting to help a young lady deal with her credit card debt. We showed her that if she made her minimum monthly payments, without any further charges, she would repay nearly three times what she had borrowed before her balance was gone. She did not realize how much more money she could have saved to use for her necessities and beyond if she had paid cash rather than paying with a credit card.

Then there was Jerome, one of my wife's former high school students who reached out for financial help. We sat down with Jerome and devised a budget for him, which looked like it would work. All went well until he signed up for a pricey cable package. When we informed him that this luxury was outside his budget, he replied, "Don't worry, I can handle it!" Only a month later he asked if we could help with his utility bill, as his power was about to be disconnected!

We have a happier story of a relative who maxed out several credit cards. He had the good fortune, however, of meeting the love of his life who agreed to marry him only on the condition he cut up all his cards. They have now been happily married for over twenty years.

Another concern involves excessive car debt. One young lady my daughter Audra mentored through the Big Brothers-Big Sisters program finally found a good job. A short time later, she was enticed into purchasing a new and expensive car. She failed to realize the monthly payments would deplete much of her income. This was income she needed for her nondiscretionary expenses. However, as luck might have it, her car was totaled at the fault of another driver and she got out from a major expense. Audra and I were able to find her a nice, old beater for a couple thousand dollars. Now this lady is managing expenses and can properly care for her young daughter.

I have seen this same scenario play out with many other young adults who were in debt over their heads due to expensive vehicle purchases. As we have helped them navigate their way out of these messes, I have developed the reputation of "used car dealer."

I would like to see our schools use financial experts to advise our students on the economic pitfalls of poor money management. After all, wouldn't most everyone like to have more money?

Some more valuable money related lessons might include the following:

- Wise use of credit cards and avoiding expensive late payments.
- The risks of playing the lottery and why it's called "the poor man's tax".
- Wise ways to purchase a home or vehicle.
- The importance of saving and investing from an early age

> *A fool and his money are soon parted.*
> —Thomas Tusser, 16th century poet

SAFETY ON THE ROAD

Given how much time we all spend in our cars, a critically important life skill is learning to be a safe driver. A few years ago, Linda and I enrolled in a safe driving course sponsored by AARP. Our insurance company gave us a premium discount upon successfully completing the course. I have little doubt the lessons learned have prevented some mishaps or at least close calls for us. As a result, I have spent many hours trying to convince others that seat belts make one many times safer, yet to this day, many still maintain that they are just as safe, if not safer, unbuckled in a car. Some have gone so far as to disable all the bells and whistles that remind them to buckle up. We probably all know of someone who would be alive today if they had only taken the time to fasten their seat belt. It took a psychological approach to convince one young man to wear his seat belt. My reasoning went like this: If you don't wear it for yourself, then just wear it for your family, because if you lose your life on the road, they will be the ones to suffer. You will be dead! My wife and I have both lost one of our closest friends this way. Surely it could be of great value to expose our school students to a professional racecar driver to explain why they should never consider skipping this safety measure.

Texting has vastly increased the hazards of distracted driving, and I often advise new drivers to expect the unexpected. We are all at the mercy of other drivers. It would likely save numerous calamities if "I will not text and drive" showed up on every New Year's resolutions list in the coming year. Some of my friends have a message programmed on their cell phones that comes up when they are driving. It says, "I can't talk now! I'm driving."

I believe most of us, as we reach our senior years, have witnessed or read of numerous tragedies where bad choices have sadly impacted lives, from unsafe driving or uninformed road safety behavior. Many have been exposed to situations where young children have been killed when they darted into the street from behind parked cars, or we hear of other times when parents severely injure their own children when backing from their garage or driveway. These are disasters that might have been avoided if the parties involved had received knowledgeable life skills in defensive driving. More than likely, these disasters haunt them for many years to come.

Other lessons topics could include:

- Winter driving cautions
- Following too closely, lane changing, and last-minute breaking

A stitch in time saves nine.
—Thomas Fuller

SAFETY AND HEALTH

Young and old alike need to be more cognizant of the threats to one's well-being that result from environmental exposure. It took too many years and many lives before we came to grips with the environmental causes of cancer. So often we would hear comments like, "My uncle smoked all his life and he lived to be ninety years old." It is sad to see, yet today, so many of our youth are learning the hard way due to their bad choices.

As an educator, I used to challenge my students to see who could come up with the longest list of environmental hazards to our health and well-being. Then as a follow-up, I would assign each student the task of researching one or more of the topics. We should not be afraid to expose our youth to the realities of life, to those who have lost their limbs, eyesight and quality of life due to poor choices regarding diet and exercise.

Aside from environmental health hazards, many other health issues harm us needlessly because young people don't—or can't—see the long-term challenges that lie ahead. Diabetes is rampant today, and most is of the type 2 variety, which is largely preventable. This insidious disease, sad to say, is becoming more and more common due to lifestyles with little exercise and poor nutrition. I have personally witnessed physical education classes where students spend the entire class sitting on the bleachers instead of getting needed exercise. If nothing more, students who are able ought to be encouraged to log a mile or two walking or running each day. According to my doctor, the best medicine he can prescribe is exercise.

Common sense is not common.
—Voltaire

A VERY HELPFUL HINT

During my first year of teaching, in the middle of the school day, I developed a nosebleed and had to stop teaching. In the teachers' lounge, a veteran teacher showed me a technique where he rolled a strip of paper into a small tube, which I then placed under my upper lip. In a short time, the bleeding stopped, and I was able to resume teaching. I was able to talk and the paper stayed in place. It was years before I had another nosebleed. This is a skill I have since used dozens of times with athletes, students, friends and family members. This life skill has never failed to work for me.

Recently, I shared this trick with one of my grandson's teammates who had a nosebleed at their game. A short time after, I received a note from the boy's mom. She said her son had chronically suffered nosebleeds but no more, thanks to the amazing solution I had shared with him.

A REQUIRED COURSE

Tuesday May 4th, 2021 is one day that will be etched in my mind for the rest of my life. My neighbor Joe has, for the past seven years, served as president of our neighborhood association. Joe and I had recently been collaborating on plans for our annual events. That was, however, until tragedy stuck.

On this particular evening Joe's wife, Sarah, ran frantically to my house, screaming desperately for my help. Sarah said Joe had fallen and was lying unconscious. She had been struggling with her cell phone and she was unable to summon an ambulance. I dialed 911 on my cell phone and proceeded to run to her home while at the same time trying to convince the 911 operator that this was a legitimate call. At their house, I found my neighbor and friend lying on their living room floor, with his arms spread apart. He did not appear to be breathing. I immediately started chest compressions with my right hand while trying to respond to a barrage of questions from the 911 operator; questions such as: "How old is he?", "Can you get him to smile?", "Can he open his eyes?" etc.

As I did my best to come up with responses to questions - most of which I had no answer for - I knew that we were losing precious time. I found myself praying for the sound of sirens.

When the paramedics arrived, they immediately took over CPR, administering chest compressions much more aggressively than what I had attempted. It looked as if they were putting their full body weight into each thrust and then trading off with a second paramedic as they tired.

After about twenty minutes, one of the paramedics came into the kitchen where Joe's wife and I were trying to call relatives. I was devastated when he told us they were not successful and Joe had died. Sara had long suffered from limited vision and depended on a walker for mobility. I thought, what a paradox of life, Joe had never needed a caregiver and yet his wife now lost hers!

Before that day in May, it had been over thirty years since I had taken any CPR courses. I read a statistic that only 3% of Americans sign up for CPR classes annually, despite it being a potentially life-saving skill. As of this writing, I have signed up for a refresher course and strongly encourage everyone to receive this critical training.. Today, many people are also eliminating their landline phones. However, if Sarah had had access to a landline phone she would have received medical assistance much sooner. Years ago, Linda and I decided to keep ours for just such emergencies. It also comes in handy when we misplace one of our cell phones!

CRITICAL THINKING

My wife, Linda, was an English major and taught history and language arts throughout her career. She has always been my reference for proper spelling and grammar. I, however, have always favored mathematics since with this discipline, I find fewer exceptions to the rules. There is also a good deal of satisfaction in problem-solving. I have always tried to encourage my students to tackle tough subjects head on, since you get further in life by completing tough tasks. In college, most courses of study have math requirements. Sadly, students often shy away from their preferred field out of their fear of mathematics. Mathematical problem-solving requires a wealth of logical reasoning, thus strengthening critical thinking skills.

Likewise, I believe debate classes strengthen critical thinking skills by having students argue a position that may be counter to their own views or what they support. One of my favorite teaching activities was an assignment where my students gave a presentation on their Most Admired Person. The students were to examine characteristics of these special people and explain what they believed made them stand out above other athletes, doctors or religious leaders. Did they use their critical thinking skills to investigate all sides of an issue and delve into the root causes of society's ills? I'm including an editorial that I submitted to our local newspaper. I used the late Senator

John McCain as someone I admired because he was often willing to "reach across the aisle." In the editorial, I cite a professional athlete who during an interview made a simple statement. He said, "What we need in the world is good political dialogue." Strengthening critical thinking skills would definitely lead to less political polarization and enhance a stronger set of values.

An editorial published in the *Peoria Journal Star* in 2020:

Put Aside our Political Games and Engage in Good, Honest Dialogue

I miss John McCain. A famous professional athlete recently said in an interview that what we need in our country is good, honest political dialogue. How much I would love to see that, to see a willingness for the powers that be to sit down unafraid to look at both sides of a problem and try to get to the root causes.

As a middle school principal, I often had situations where a student, parent or teacher would come with a problem where we both struggled to find a solution. However, when we put together a team of teachers, parents and support personnel, good things usually happened.

I realize how fortunate I have been to not just being a citizen of the United States, but to have had the good fortune of circumstance. Tom Brokaw, former NBC Evening News Anchor, once said, "I did not get to where I am today without a lot of help along the way." I am convinced that if we would all walk in other's shoes for a while, we might see the world quite differently.

It's time to put aside our political games and engage in good, honest dialogue. We have some serious issues to resolve.

Following the example of Sen. John McCain, Let's reach across the aisle.

Gary Millen

I am not alone in my perspective that critical thinking skills could help improve our political dialogue. Minnesota Senator Amy Klobuchar, who sought the 2020 nomination for President on the Democratic ticket, has emphasized the importance of this life skill. During several interviews she stated that one of our biggest problems in government is the lack of critical thinking. If only more of our leaders had used their influence and power early in the pandemic surely the impact would have been much less severe.

As a middle school teacher and sometimes almost a "preacher," I tried to impress upon my students the importance of taking a courageous stand and speaking out when they saw injustices and the need for change in our communities and world. I wish we could see much more of this important life skill. I was quite proud when one of my former students shared an editorial he was submitting to our local newspaper in the spring of 2020. The following submission epitomizes the result of one person's use of critical thinking.

An editorial submitted to the *Peoria Journal Star* in the spring of 2020:

Common Sense Isn't Common

> *I'm angry. I'm angry because I see so many lives across our country being lost needlessly to the COVID-19 virus. I am angry when I see that other countries, like South Korea, have had much more success addressing this pandemic due to their rapid response. They got the genetic code for the virus from China and quickly developed a test. Then they did massive testing with a citizenry that was willing to comply with wearing masks and sheltering in place.*
>
> *Dr. Anthony Fauci, director of the National Institute of Allergy and Infectious Diseases, (NIAID), being as diplomatic as he can be, said our response was a failing partly due to the pushbacks that were occurring in February and March. Who was pushing back? I think we all know.*
>
> *Our president said, "I take no responsibility at all." Former President Truman might have said, "The buck stops here!"*
>
> *All our past presidents have defended the media and proclaimed how important the media is to the preservation of our democracy. Perhaps if we allowed ourselves to be better enlightened, common sense could once again rule.*
>
> *We have friends in the medical profession who are telling us they are still without adequate*

personal protective equipment (PPE). They see their colleagues coming to work in fear of contracting the virus and even more afraid of carrying it back home to their loved ones.

I believe the pandemic was bound to come to the United States, but I also believe had we implemented our mitigation in timely manner, many people would still be alive today.

Dr. Fauci also said it would have been nice if we still had our federal pandemic response unit, which was abolished in 2018. Perhaps such a unit would have helped us heed the early warnings about the virus.

Yes, fellow Americans, I'm very angry, and I believe you should be, too.

—Anonymous

RELATIONSHIPS

Bullying has always been a problem in schools, and with social media, this problem has increased dramatically because bullies have even more outlets from which to attack. While this issue has gotten more attention in recent years, there is much more we can do to address it.

As a middle school principal, I placed a great deal of emphasis on addressing bullies in the classroom, lunchroom, lab or playground. Many years ago as a middle school student, I remember having a class where one of our requirements was to pair up and interview a different classmate each day. Then we were asked to share something special we had learned about our partner with the rest of the class. As a result of these simple conversations, we cultivated healthier relationships and concern for each other; sure enough, bullying never seemed to be a problem.

Social interactions could do much to help all of us deal with emotions, such as jealousy, that keep us from being our best selves. Through these social interactions, we can practice self-reflection and ask ourselves questions such as, "Why are we often envious of others?" "Is this a logical emotion?" "Does it really hurt me if someone else's child makes the honor roll?" The answers to these and the self-awareness they provide might stifle those sinister emotions we all wrestle with at some point in our lives.

Throughout my life and in my career, I have been blessed to adopt new role models. An acquaintance of mine who is a retired Caterpillar executive is someone I have always admired from afar. He created an ethics policy that he implements with his family. When his children were young, he would have them recite the family ethics code each night. The code dealt with their pledge on how to treat others. They grew to know and live that code, and it has helped them throughout their rich lives.

This same executive's father-in-law also taught me a great deal about positive interactions with others. I taught with Dale for twenty years and he became a close friend. As I was coaching math teams, coaching sports teams and receiving affirmations, several of which I probably did not deserve, Dale was always close by cheering for my success. I thought about how unique it was for Dale to find pleasure when others were winning. I lost my good friend a few years ago, but I know that I am a better person because of his selfless example.

Several years ago, my siblings and I collaborated on a plan to help bring our families closer. We decided to hold an annual family reunion each summer on the Saturday before Father's Day. Over the past several years, we agreed to hold our reunions at our retirement home near Peoria. The home is our second residence where we have a nice two-bedroom house, seven wooded acres and a small, stocked fishpond. A close friend caters our food. He is an entrepreneur and struggling restaurant owner who appreciates the business. I have been glad to pick up the tab for the catering, as it's one of the best investments of $400–$500 I can make. Over the years,

I've received several thank you notes from nieces and nephews for helping them reconnect with their aunts, uncles and cousins.

These are simply a few of the stories and memories that are etched in my mind. In the following chapters, I hope to share many more happenings that are revelations of how a positive and proactive approach to human relationships can enrich our lives.

MUSIC AND THE GOLDEN YEARS

The "golden years" are not always golden. In the words of the famous actress, Betty Davis, "Old age is not for sissies."

For many years, Linda and I had enjoyed traveling with several other couples, visiting varied attractions across the Midwest. These travels included many musical performances. For the most part, these trips together have come to an end as the challenges of aging limits mobility for many of our friends. Some of these friends are no longer with us. Most of the others now find comfort in nursing or retirement communities. In spite of our happy memories, we have our lonely days and miss the fun times we shared for so many years.

Recently, I decided to take a proactive approach. If we could no longer go to the music, why not bring the music to us?

A couple of years ago, I began compiling an array of music videos. Some are contemporary and many feature country songs that we heard live over the years. We are now meeting in small numbers in various homes for music concerts of our own making.

We are now meeting more frequently and the number of people involved seems to be increasing. Some of our members are now joining in singing along with the videos. The enthusiasm is growing, and few seem to worry about how they sound. The beauty is in the music and the memories it brings.

For as long as I am able, I hope to continue promoting these musical get-to-gethers and hope to expand my outreach. We feel that music is a "spice of life" with a therapeutic effect.

While an evening discussing politics can often have a divisive result, an evening of beautiful music is always uplifting. My friends usually tell me they're ready for the next sing-a-long any time!

OUR PROUD TALE

A few years ago, at Golda Meir School in Milwaukee, Wisconsin, a parent walked into the principal's office with some good news to share. She said, "Up until recently, my son hated to come to school. Then a classmate asked his teacher if my son could be his partner and be seated next to him. Now he looks forward to coming to school due to his new special friend."

Several hundred miles away, another young student was being shunned and bullied because of symptoms of autism. Then one classmate reached out and invited him for a weekend sleepover. This gesture has made all the difference as the boy with autism has now become accepted by most of his classmates. I'm proud to say that both of these caring young boys are our grandsons. In the spirit of fostering positive relationships, I would hope that every parent and child could see an inspiring movie called *Wonder*, which tells a story of a student bullied because of a physical defect. It will touch your heart.

SELF-ESTEEM

A sad statistic tells us that a high proportion of men of color will at some time in their life be incarcerated. There's no doubt, these same young men have the potential to make wonderful contributions to society. I marvel when I see so many young athletes perform amazing feats with a basketball or football. Yet, I can't help but wonder what will become of their lives ten years later, especially when the cheering stops. Will they be putting that athletic scholarship to good use or even collecting a multimillion-dollar salary as a professional athlete? As we all have seen, it is typical for young males when asked about career plans to respond, "I want to be a professional athlete when I grow up!"

Several years ago, a mother of two of my students asked to share a life story with me. She said she came from a large family, yet she was the only one of all her siblings who had not been incarcerated sometime in their life. More importantly, however, she said she believed she knew why she was spared. She said when she was in primary school, she had a teacher named Mrs. Marks who became her mentor. Every time she was tempted to do something wrong, she would think "Mrs. Marks would not like that!" I shared her story with many of my teacher friends to let them see how powerful their influence could be. As a teacher, I have often had parents relate things that I have said or done that boosted their child's self-esteem.

Statements like, "Mr. Millen said I asked an excellent question" or "Coach Millen said if everyone played as hard as I did, we would have won that game!"

I sincerely believe that every child needs at least one person in their life they look up to and would never want to disappoint.

People will soon forget what you said, people will soon forget what you did, but they will never forget how you made them feel.
—Maya Angelou

PLEASE LET ME BOAST

My wife Linda and I are grateful and proud that we have always made an extra effort to stay close to our parents, siblings and other relatives. As a bonus, we have been blessed to have the most family-oriented and loving son and daughter we could have ever hoped for. Even better, they both found spouses who are truly "keepers" and fantastic parents to our four wonderful grandchildren.

My son, Vince, and his family live in a nice subdivision in Eureka, Missouri. Their neighbors call Vince the "ambassador of the neighborhood." I cannot imagine anyone having more friends than Vince. He still stays in close contact with former neighbors and classmates from fifty years ago. He has always been the glue that keeps family and friends together. As a food and beverage manager, he successfully uses his diplomatic talents. It is not at all unusual to get a call late in the evening as our son makes his twenty-mile trek home from work. He'll say, "Just checking to see if you are okay. Love you!" And what great parents Vince and his wife, Traci, have been. Over the past fourteen years, they have opened their home to two of our talented grandsons.

Our daughter, Audra, had the misfortune, or I hope good fortune, of having her parents for teachers. In high school, she excelled in all her subjects and was focusing on a course of study in the physical sciences. At that time,

Bradley University offered career counseling sessions and Audra took part at our urging. The recommended results led us to enroll her in a program titled, "Mathematical Methods in the Social Sciences" at Northwestern University. Upon her graduation, she had no trouble getting job interviews. Ultimately, Audra ended up crunching numbers for the Congressional Budget Office in Washington, D.C.

Today, Audra lives in Milwaukee with her husband, Joel, who at the time of my writing this book was the Secretary of the Department of Administration for the State of Wisconsin. They are the proud parents of two more of our brilliant grandchildren, Allison and Conor. Audra and Joel have instilled a love of learning, especially math, in their children's daily lives.

Linda and I have compiled a book in our home that we call, "My Quotable Grandkids." Some of our favorite quotes and stories show how they were mastering math at an early age. When our granddaughter was about four, due to some misunderstanding, I'm sure, she was sent to "time out" by her mother for a five-minute discipline. She was told that the five minutes would be cut in half if she was good. Allison quickly responded to that deal by saying, "Mom, you can't cut five in half; it's an odd number!" My high school algebra students sometimes struggled with the concept of consecutive odd integers.

Around the age of five, Allison's younger brother, Conor, loved to show us his number skills with a phone call to Peoria. "Grandma, would you like to hear me count to 100 by fives?" "Grandpa, would you like to hear me count to 100 by sevens?" Conor was also showing some interest in probability at about that same age. He flipped a penny in the air and said to his dad, "What would you like, heads or toes?"

I'm sure my wife deserves ninety-five per cent of the credit for keeping our children and grandchildren so close. When they get an opportunity to come to our home in Peoria, the grandkids get lots of laughs and enjoyment reading their famous quotes from years gone by. The most hilarious quote is R-rated and came from grandson Michael at the age of five. I'm saving that whopper for a later time.

OUR BEST TEACHERS

An important lesson in life is that we should never be afraid to learn from our children. What a blessing it turned out to be that both of our children were exposed to diversity throughout their school experiences. Through their involvement in school sports teams, our son, Vince, and daughter, Audra, had teammates of various races, religions and ethnicities. Many times, they witnessed the ugly face of racism and prejudices from the other side. As a result of our children's experiences, Linda and I were exposed to a diverse group of friends and the parents of their friends on our travels, at school events and often in our own home.

Vince, Audra and their wonderful spouses have made it a requirement to expose our four grandchildren to diverse experiences to this day. Because I felt inspired by Vince, Audra and our four loving grandchildren, I was motivated to submit the following editorial on racism, which was published in our local newspaper in September of 2020.

An Editorial published in the *Peoria Journal Star* in the summer of 2020:

A Smile, Wave or Hello Could Help

My life has been enriched by the fact that I've spent many years involved with the inner city of Peoria through social agencies, teaching, mentoring and living in a diverse neighborhood. When I see a person of color, I see a good person. I see someone I would like to know. I see a person just like me who wants the same things out of life that I do, and if I'm lucky enough to get to know that person I am always right. Sadly, though, we have very good people involved in law enforcement who too often are only involved with people of color when there is a problem, and the reverse is true in that the only time they see the police is when there is a problem.

Are we developing too many of our opinions from second-hand information? I have close friends who have unapologetically confessed that they are racist. However, racism is illogical. No one deserves to be judged by the color of their skin. In the words of well-known educator Jane Elliott, "God created one race... that's the human race."

I just wonder what might change if we all made a concerted effort to communicate with people of every ethnicity we see every day. Perhaps a hello, wave or just a smile would lead to a hello, wave or smile in return.

Gary Millen

TUTORING

My first tutoring experience occurred in the spring of 1965. I was in my first year of teaching at Roosevelt Junior High School in Peoria, Illinois. The request came from a school administrator whose son was failing algebra. As a first-year teacher, my beginning salary was meager, so I was looking forward to the extra income. When I quoted my price of five dollars per session, I was told my rate was excessive. However, that was the last time I heard any complaint, as I continued to tutor their son weekly for the next two years in algebra and chemistry.

Tutoring can be a godsend for a struggling student who, more than anything, needs a boost in confidence. One of the greatest benefits from tutoring is that the tutor is better able to access the student's understanding on a consistent basis and thus make considerable progress each session. It has always amazed me how often parents will spend hundreds of dollars on expensive toys but hesitate to invest where it will do the greatest good.

Another very memorable tutoring request came from a close friend who was working with a special education student. The Special Services Coordinator told my friend that Sarah was so low functioning that she would always be a nonreader. Yet my friend had taught her to read and now was asking me to help with her math. My first couple of sessions with Sarah were futile, and I was ready to throw in the towel. Then, when I was hardly looking, Sarah began to achieve. This was when I first came to understand that all kids can learn but maybe not all at the same pace. Many years later I ran into Sarah. She was gainfully employed, happily married and had recently received her Associates Degree from our local community college.

Recently, a church associate shared a concern for his third-grade nephew who was behind in math and having discipline problems in school. I offered my services, and he brought Jason to my house a few days later. My church friend decided to sit in on my first session with Jason and quickly concluded that I would have my hands full if I wished to continue. Jason found every possible distraction in the room to avoid the subject matter. In the next session, I decided to use a different approach by incorporating several games that involved numbers. Even though some games were quite challenging, I found Jason to be very bright. He memorized his multiplication tables in a couple of sessions. I used a method with which I have found much success and have used with several other students over the years. I will explain this technique in a later chapter.

I'll never forget a couple of remarks Jason made during our sessions. First, he told me the reason he had done so well with his multiplication tables is that he was cheating. He said, "I memorized them!" This was just what I wanted to hear. At the conclusion of another lesson, Jason said, "Mr. Millen, you're more like a friend than a teacher!" I'm happy to report that Jason is now doing well in school.

A few years ago, I decided I needed more time to myself and so I cut back on my tutoring. I decided to raise my rate by five dollars thinking that would do the trick. I added three new customers as a result!

MENTORING

I f I had to describe the one program of which I am most proud, it would involve mentoring middle school students. In the seven years of my tenure as a principal at Calvin Coolidge Middle School, we recruited over one hundred volunteers from the Peoria area. These mentors consisted of Bradley University basketball players (men and women), Bradley students from human development classes, retired teachers and recruits from senior citizen organizations. All volunteers went through an orientation seminar provided by Peoria Public Schools.

Many of the mentors worked right inside the classroom. Teachers who used manipulatives and required lots of hands-on lessons for their students benefited the most from having mentors working in their classrooms. We also had a designated "community room" where mentors would assist students with their studies.

One of my main concerns at the onset of the mentoring program was that it might be considered a negative to be assigned a mentor. This fear was quickly dispelled when several students started requesting mentors. On one memorable occasion, I had a young lady whisper in my ear saying, "Mr. Millen, do I have to have a problem before I can get one of these mentors?"

In 2001, after thirty-seven years in public education, I retired. To stay connected and continue working with young people, I went through the formal training I mentioned earlier at the Children's Home in Peoria to become a respite worker. My first assignment was Evan, a second grader who was struggling at school. He was particularly negative about reading and he was becoming a discipline problem. His single mother had three other young children and was reaching out for help with Evan. I immediately enrolled Evan in the public library's summer reading program and took him to the Lincoln branch facility three days each week. The first couple of visits did not go well as he balked at reading with me. That's when I took a gamble. I offered Evan one dollar for every book he would read with me. Before long, we were reading three or four books and Evan was making big bucks at my expense. I was curious about what Evan was doing with his money. To my great surprise—and joy—he was giving it to his mother to put gasoline in her car. He once asked me if I knew how much it would cost to get the fuel gauge all the way to the F (full mark). I believe Evan would have done most anything to help his mother!

I remained in contact with Evan for several years. I could usually expect a call from him on report card day. He knew I would reward him financially for good grades. That was probably the best gas money I ever spent.

THE REWARDS OF ALTRUISM

Helping and caring for others may add years to one's life, according to many articles about health and longevity. From an early age, no day ever felt complete if I could not look back with a feeling of accomplishment. I felt even better when I knew I had made life better for my friends and family.

Our father always pushed my siblings and me to work in our fields or address the never-ending needs of maintaining or upgrading our home. Many times, we complied reluctantly. I recall one Easter hearing one of my brothers complaining, "Today is Easter! Why do we have to work on a holiday?"

Often the tasks my siblings and I worked on were not of the highest quality when completed. We had cheap materials, old tools and no training. My oldest brother, Erwin, was a somewhat self-taught auto mechanic and electrician. Later in life, I knew I could always call on him for advice. For years, we did a good deal of concrete work as we constructed our own well pit, septic tank, basement floors and sidewalks. We hauled all our sand and gravel from creek beds that fed into the Mississippi River. As the youngest boy, my job was operating the mixer for all the concrete we used. Looking back, it is unnerving to know that we got by with far less than true quality. Our well was never properly sealed. The septic system often overflowed into the front lawn, and we never thought to apply for the required building permits.

During one of our building projects, we added an entire entry foyer to the lower level of our house. To save money, we used lightweight lamp cord to wire some of the lights and outlets. This worked until many years later when we installed an air-conditioner in a nearby window. I hoped this would give my mother some relief during the hot summer months. All was well until we saw smoke pouring from a roof vent. The fire department was quickly called to save our house. The lamp cord was not constructed to meet the electrical demands of the air-conditioner. This was when I first came to realize the importance of building codes.

On one other occasion, the fire department came to our rescue when our brush fire burned out of control and threatened to spread to the six houses that were adjacent to our property. We learned a great deal through trial and error, but the errors could have cost us our home—and ruined plenty of friendships!

Lumbering was another common activity, since regular trimming was necessary and sometimes large trees needed to be removed. A tree died near the front of our house and leaned perilously close to the entrance, a clear sign that it needed to be removed. We attached a long rope to a main branch as high into the tree as we could reach. My job was to pull the tree away from the house as brother Jack sawed through the lower trunk. Everything was going fine as I pulled the tree in my direction and the cut that Jack had made began to give way. In a split second, disaster nearly struck as my rope snapped and the tree swung back toward the house. I vividly remember the startled look on my mother's face as the tree teetered in her direction. This may have been the day I truly started to believe in a God, because my quick prayer to save the house was answered. To this day, I still do not know what kept the tree from going all the way down and crushing the front of the house. We quickly called on professionals to complete this dangerous task!

We economized by using salvaged firewood to supplement heating our home. A long, two-man saw was used to cut the larger logs into small pieces that would fit into our furnace. I spent many hours pulling on my end of the two-man saw.

Thanks to my father and older brothers, I developed a work ethic that is part of my psyche to this day. Even now, I find each day of my life more fulfilling when I can look back with the knowledge that I have accomplished something significant. This is particularly true when I know I've helped others who need it. Some truck owners have a bumper sticker that says, "Yes, this is my truck, and no I will not help you move!" You will never see such a sticker on my truck!

Years ago, I became involved with inner-city agencies, such as the Children's Home and Peoria Common Place. Aside from mentoring, I was often asked to deliver furniture to needy families. These deliveries often turned challenging as we might have to remove part of a door frame to get a couch through the main door.

One of the more memorable occasions took place when I helped deliver and hook up a donated clothes washer. Everything went well until the recipient insisted that we lift the appliance so she could straighten the rug beneath. When we raised the washer, the inlet hose snapped off the faucet and water began gushing down the hallway. At first, the occupant did not know how to shut off the water supply. When we located the shut off valve, her husband was not able to turn it in order to stop the torrent of water. By putting my thumb over the break, I was able to hold back the stream until a wrench was found. Thanks to prior experience with plumbing, I was able to make the necessary repair. A quick trip to a nearby hardware store for a new faucet, PVC pipe and cement supplied the necessities.

It bothers me to see needy people with property damages that demand attention. I enjoy helping others. Still, I'm always relieved when the tasks are done. Many of these jobs involve replacing windows and broken doors. Much of this damage is due to domestic violence situations.

One episode involved the grandparent of one of the young people I was mentoring. Grandma Mary had adopted several children during her younger years. Her youngest, Robby, developed schizophrenia and presented a number of challenges. Robby would often run through the house chasing make-believe villains. I attempted to help whenever I could by replacing broken windows, patching holes in walls and replacing doors that Robby had destroyed.

Mary sought help for Robby. After two hearings in front of a courthouse judge, much documentation and record keeping, we acquired social security insurance, along with the necessary medical treatment for Robby. Robby is now in his twenties, employed and fully functioning. I have never known a nicer young man. Mary happily states, "I now have my son back!"

On the other hand, I consider my mentoring with Mary's grandson, Donald, less than a success. On one of our times together, Donald accompanied me to a US Cellular store. I was unaware that Donald had taken one of the store's expensive cell phones. A phone call from the store threatening my mentee's arrest let me know that I wasn't getting through to him as I had hoped I could. I immediately returned to the phone store to pay a tidy sum for the missing phone. Then I went to find Donald. Luckily, I recovered the stolen phone when I observed him hiding it under the evergreen shrubs in front of Mary's house. Since then, Donald has had some good days and yet other negative involvements. I'm still hoping for better behaviors.

Peoria Common Place was a non-profit agency that exposed me to the challenges of the inner city. During the mid-1970s, I agreed to serve as treasurer for Common Place. This position involved reconciling bank accounts, writing checks and handling required distributions to the federal government. Back then, I used a hand cranked machine to total amounts.

One of the Common Place directors had acquired a million-dollar grant that focused on rehabilitating ex-convicts. These men were taught construction skills and worked repairing and upgrading homes on Peoria's South Side. Every Friday afternoon, these men would be waiting for me at the Common Place facility. At that time, I distributed the paychecks for their week's work. Not surprisingly, I always had one hundred per cent participation on that day. It is hard to explain how rewarding it is to know that your life has real value because you have bettered the lives of others. As a teacher and mentor, I have always tried to involve youth in civic activity. Visiting shut-ins, delivering Christmas baskets and neighborhood clean-up tasks are such examples. Often these young people would return from a project inspired to become further involved with helping those in need.

MOTIVATIONAL STRATEGIES

M otivation is one of the greatest gifts we can provide to young people and I believe all kids can be motivated if we are creative in our approaches. People laugh when I tell them that three of my most effective educators were my library manager, band teacher and custodian. On more than one occasion when a student was sent to the office for discipline, they would tell me the only reason they came to school was because the band teacher or the custodian needed them. The band teacher and custodian didn't always see it the same way, however. Although they helped with tasks around the school, the more challenging students at times made it more difficult for these school personnel to complete their work. However, these adults were still willing to go out of their way to help a struggling student find purpose by helping others.

My library manager also went out of her way to help inspire students and she worked wonders. Many a morning, I would observe students waiting by the library door to be the first to obtain a copy of the novel she had promoted the day before. Some library managers across the school district were negative regarding the Accelerated Reader (AR) program, which is designed to motivate, monitor and manage a student's reading practice. Once they have finished a book, students take a computer comprehension quiz and earn AR points depending on the difficulty of the book. At Calvin Coolidge, we would convert the AR points into AR "bucks". At the end of the school year students would be invited to an AR auction at which they could bid on prizes using their AR "bucks". It should be noted that these prizes were donated by local businesses.

Like other programs, however, the success or failure had more to do with the salesperson. I'll never, never forget the day I walked into the library and observed the library manager's Accelerated Reader "Hall of Fame" posted on the wall. Two of her top readers were students that I had up for suspension just weeks earlier. My library manager reached out to teachers, staff members and parents for their participation in the AR program in order to help engage and inspire each student to reach their reading goal. As the school principal, I learned to keep my distance, however, after the custodian obtained a higher score than I did on one of the tests.

As I worked with teachers at Calvin Coolidge and later in retirement, I shared evaluation techniques that I had used in the classroom. One of my most successful strategies to motivate involved grading. All my grades were based on a multiple of 5. Daily homework received a score of 0, 5 or 10; quizzes were worth 25 points and tests earned 50 or 100. I kept a daily running tally in my grade book. Being based on 5, I could quickly tally each student's total. At the end of each week, I would post student point totals on preprinted class rosters. A new grade scale was posted at the top so students could see how many points it took to attain an A, B, C, D or F. Often, I would hear students exclaim, "You mean if I had turned in my homework yesterday, I would now have a B?" Having these weekly rosters of grades came in handy in dealing with parents who would say that their child did not know they were doing poorly. On the contrary, they knew their status weekly, and I could quickly show the parent the copies of my postings.

As a middle school principal, I always encouraged my teachers to greet the students as they got off the bus, walked the halls or entered their classroom. They were sometimes surprised how something so simple could be so important. One day a student even commented, "Mr. Jones, you forgot to say hi to me this morning."

I still remember over sixty years ago hearing my teacher telling another teacher what a great student I was! I suspect now that he purposely wanted me to overhear his comment. If his actions were intentional, they had their desired impact, because from that day on, I tried my best to never have him change his opinion of me.

TAKING RISKS

Often, I've been advised and inclined not to go in the direction of the greatest risk. However, maybe foolishly, I believe we should all take risks at times. I hope never to be so secure that I can hardly move, so secure that I cannot make a difference, especially when difference is needed. One particularly moving poem is, "The Road Not Taken" by Robert Frost. I identify with his words: "Two roads diverged in a wood, and I—I took the one less traveled by; and that made all the difference."

In the spring of 1993, three principal vacancies were opening for the ensuing school year. I was honored to have the option of accepting any one of the three. Even though Calvin Coolidge Middle School presented the greatest challenges, I also believed this choice also offered the greatest possibilities. I chose the principalship at Calvin Coolidge.

Having chosen the principalship at Calvin Coolidge made all the difference. At Coolidge, I found teachers who were willing to buy into a philosophy of "teaming". I found teachers who were willing to go the extra mile to implement programs that often went way beyond the typical school day. I found teachers who were willing to enroll in in-service classes and summer workshops, and just as importantly, teachers who were willing to take risks for the betterment of their students.

Many of our programs involved giving students ownership of their own education. Some students were involved in tutoring other students in our after-school study club. One teacher welcomed Bradley University students into her classroom to assist with hands-on activities.

In my second year as principal, I took a risk where I even surprised myself. Two seventh grade boys had been held back a grade level in a previous school year and were still struggling socially and academically. We presented the following challenge to both. I told each boy that we would consider moving them up to the next grade level on the condition that they achieve grades of B or higher on their next and final report cards. They both proudly came through! When we checked on their progress the following year, we found both having a happy and successful year as high school freshmen. I must confess, however, that this entire risky scheme was the idea of one of my master teachers, not me!

Not all my attempts at risk taking were successful. Nine years ago, Linda launched Rising Stars, a very successful after school tutoring program through our church, University United Methodist Church (UUMC) in Peoria, Illinois. As part of Peoria Public Schools' Adopt-A-School program, UUMC adopted Thomas Jefferson School, and volunteers from UUMC tutor and mentor students at the school for ninety minutes every Tuesday. The tutors are paired with the same Rising Star student each week to develop a relationship between student and tutor. Healthy snacks and recreation are also built into the Rising Stars program. UUMC's Rising Stars program was recognized by the Peoria Public School Board as one of the initiatives that has made a significant impact on students at Thomas Jefferson. Our local newspaper, the *Peoria Journal Star*, also did an in-depth feature on Rising Stars.

Several years ago, I was volunteering with one of the Rising Stars students who was making much progress in his academic achievement. He shared with me that he had been held back in an earlier grade and would love to be caught up with his original classmates to avoid being looked down upon as a failure. Research tells us that, next to losing a loved one, students grieve the most about failing a grade.

Brad was moving to a different school within Peoria Public Schools, so we felt it would be an excellent opportunity to pursue moving him to his original grade. I met with the principal of the school he would be attending. I even promised to work with him over the summer to help address any deficiencies he would need. Unfortunately, our request was denied, and Brad was not afforded the opportunity to regain his lost dignity.

I still regret not further pursuing this loss on Brad's behalf.

An important aspect of our philosophy at Calvin Coolidge was to provide an educational climate that was physically and emotionally safe. We put a great deal of emphasis on combating bullying. In our attempts to get to the bottom of a particular issue and deal with the facts, we had to have the trust of our students. When the students knew they could trust authority, they were much more willing to confide in us when they were aware of impending problems. As a result, several serious incidents were avoided when students knew they were not going to suffer repercussions for being a "snitch". On two occasions, serious incidents were surely avoided when students warned of weapons being brought to school.

Following is an editorial that I submitted to the *Peoria Journal Star* in 2002. The subject of the editorial was a teacher and coach whose life modeled the value of positivity.

Good Teachers Focus on Students' Strengths, not Weaknesses

Recently, Peoria lost a good friend. Dale White was a dedicated teacher, coach and mentor to our inner-city youth for nearly fifty years. Those who knew him well know there are literally hundreds of Peorians, young and old, whose lives were influenced and whose paths were redirected by the influence of this one man.

Coach White was able to create successful programs in track, softball and basketball, often in the most challenging settings. Our public schools are challenged to pay for the cost of maintaining and upgrading the educational system. These expenditures will fail to produce expected results without the human element that comes from the love and encouragement that only a caring individual can deliver.

In the fall of 1999, I recruited Dale White to coach the girls' softball team at Calvin Coolidge Middle School. Needless to say, he gave tenfold. Although his teams were seldom undefeated, at the end of every season each team member felt like a champion. He could go head-to-head with the most difficult student, but when the confrontation was over the student would come out feeling like a winner. No students wanted to disappoint Coach White because he let them know every day how special they were.

There are many teachers in the Peoria area, like Mr. White, who are winning kids every day by building on their strengths instead of their weaknesses. We need to support these teachers and encourage adults to lead from the model set by Dale White.

Gary Millen

You miss 100% of the shots you don't take.
    —Wayne Gretzky

A SUCCESS STORY

During my first year as a middle school principal, I implemented a year-end, two-day trip to St. Louis as a reward to the eighth-grade students for their good behavior. A Friday-Saturday trip was permitted by the school district as long as our Friday portion could be considered educational. The agenda included a visit to the St Louis Science Center and the Omnimax show on Friday. Friday evening included swimming at the Holidome with a pizza party around the pool. Our entire Saturday was dedicated to fun at Six Flags.

The first trip was a learning experience. Even though the kids had a good time, we had to deal with a few issues. These included the kids wanting to stay up all night, others complaining that the Science Center was boring, and lastly, a few opting out of the trip altogether. We chose to use a proactive approach to these issues. To address the boredom, we created a scavenger hunt for the Science Center with cash rewards for their successful discoveries. Swimming in the afternoon, followed by an Omnimax show, and more swimming in the evening solved the problem of staying up late. Saturday morning included a stop at McDonalds on our way to Six Flags. We made sure to have a few extra envelopes of cash for the two or three students who would choose to stay on the bus due to a lack of funds for their meals.

After our first year, none of the next year's graduates chose to stay back. This was particularly true after, as seventh graders, they heard the eighth graders talk about all the fun they had! Other teachers were amazed that we also included the eighth-grade students from our BD (behavioral disorder) class who made sure to improve their behavior so they could be included. Even more astounding was the fact that the BD kids were probably the best behaved on the trip. I don't think they were accustomed to people going out of the way for them and thus they appreciated this memorable opportunity.

Programs like the one just described require considerable initial effort and then continuing attention and enhancement. Some of my colleagues would look at several of the programs in this book and call them "fluff" and say they are not worth the trouble or the risks for the betterment of our students. I cannot think of a single activity described herein that was not worth the effort and which I'm not proud to share.

An Editorial in the Peoria Journal Star in 1995:

Want Quality Education? It's at Peoria Schools

District 150 has received so much bad press in the last few months; I think it is important for the community and surrounding areas to know that District 150 has several schools which are doing an outstanding job of not only educating the children, but meeting the many other needs which children have, namely emotional and social. Calvin Coolidge is one of those schools.

Because I am a teacher with children in the Peoria School District, and an active member of two PTAs, I feel that I am a fairly good judge. Gary Millen and his faculty are interested in educating the whole child and it shows in the many extracurricular activities, as well as the day-to-day curriculum.

Student Council, Mathcounts, Scholars' Cup, Odyssey of the Mind, Science Club, intramural sports and open gym (to ward off after school off-season boredom) are just a few of the activities offered. There is also an after school tutoring program, a tutoring program in coordination with senior citizens and a mentoring program with Bradley students for children with special needs.

The Coolidge teachers and people in the community are presently in the process of planning the development of an exercise trail, a prairie, a butterfly garden, a vegetable garden and new landscaping, all on the school premises, due to a grant which has been written by Mr. Millen and the faculty.

It is very important to understand that these teachers do what they do because they are professional, dedicated teachers. Many of them are receiving no or minimal extra pay for the extra hours of work they are doing for our children.

There is quality education going on here in Peoria, and everyone needs to realize it.

Calvin Coolidge Parent

THE POWER OF ROLE MODELS

everal years ago, Linda and I had the distinct pleasure of attending ex-president Jimmy Carter's Sunday school class at the Maranatha Baptist Church in Plains, Georgia. We consider this one of the highlights of our lives, even though neither of us voted for him in 1976 or 1980. I know he may not go down in history as one of our greatest presidents, but I do feel he will be remembered as one of the best ex-presidents based on all he has done to eradicate disease and monitor elections in countries around the globe.

Despite his vast knowledge of the Bible, President Carter openly states he is not a religious man, but a man of faith. It bothers me immensely when I see people using religious doctrine as their basis to discriminate against others. It is easy to look down on others who don't always cater to our standards of behavior. As a young teacher in a depressed inner-city school, I often faced tough challenges with disruptive students. When teachers sometimes wanted to give up on a student, our principal at the time would remind us, "There but for the grace of God go you or I!" I sincerely believe that had I been raised in the same situation as many of my first students, I could very well have made many of the same wrong choices. I never forget that I did not get to where I am today without many breaks in life and without the inspiration of those who served as positive role models. These role models were siblings, teachers, my parents, and inspirational people like President Carter.

At times, it seems easy to believe that those who live in the "bad" part of town, those who look or talk differently, those who live in places that seem so different from what I am used to—Russia, Iran or Africa—could not be anything like me. Would it not be enlightening if we could just walk in their shoes for a day or two? We might find that we're a lot more alike and have the same hopes and dreams. Wouldn't we see a different way of caring for each other? Wouldn't we be more likely to address real problems in a proactive instead of a reactive way?

There is little that is more rewarding in life than helping others as much and as often as we can. Early in my teaching career, I found I had a lot more success when I treated my students firmly but fairly. I always attempted to deal with even the most difficult student in a respectful manner and resist the temptation to attack them verbally.

One of my teacher colleagues had a sign on her classroom door that read, "Kindness Spoken Here". Maybe if all of us—our elected leaders included—tried employing greater kindness and respect we just might be able to reverse the plight of divisiveness that has truly infected our world.

I'm thankful that throughout my youth I was exposed to good books and media. I was also influenced by older siblings who were powerful role models. My late brother Erwin spent his entire life doing volunteer work, organizing food pantries, serving on school boards and, ultimately, becoming the first recipient of the Joe Brown East Moline Volunteer Award. After Hurricane

Katrina, he enticed Linda and me into multiple trips to New Orleans to restore homes and bring hope to families.

My older sister, Vanetta, and my younger sister, Margene, both lived extensively in Florida. Similarly, during their retirement years, they developed a similar routine. Each day, they would make their rounds checking on the well-being of neighbors and friends. Margene continues this humanitarian practice today.

On several occasions, I had the honor of being asked to give a commencement speech for one of our middle schools. I found this to be an excellent opportunity to impress upon the audience the importance of their presence that night and their value as role models throughout these graduates' lives.

EMPOWERING STUDENTS FOR LIFE

I n this chapter, I will describe some of the strategies I observed that empowered students. Many years ago, my daughter had a math teacher in high school who was one of the most conscientious and hard-working I've ever seen. What bothered me about him, however, is that most of his teaching was algorithmic. His goal was to program his students so that they would be able to complete their homework. On the flip side is what is called "empowering students" or teaching more "conceptually". I always told my students that I did not want to transform them into human calculators, since calculators will always be faster and are extremely accurate.

In the early 1990s when I was serving as a math staff developer for the Peoria Public Schools, I was privileged to observe excellent teaching and then share successful methods across the district. On one occasion, I was invited by an inner-city teacher to observe a math project her class had completed. I was surprised to find that the project was on the fourth floor and her third-grade class was housed in the basement. When she suggested we go upstairs to see the project, I asked who was going to supervise her class while we were gone. She assured me not to worry. It was at least fifteen minutes before we returned from the fourth floor to the basement classroom. To my surprise, her room was all in order. The students had completed, collected and filed the day's assignments; this was a beautiful example of what can happen when students are given ownership!

Giving students more ownership in classroom activities is an effective way of teaching. Instead of having students complete an assignment by answering assigned questions, I would require my students to submit a question on that week's lesson. Then I would often use their question on the next test or quiz. Their parents would sometimes hear, "Mom! Dad! Mr. Millen used my question on this week's test!"

I observed other teachers who required every student to maintain a journal, which was kept in the classroom. During the last five or ten minutes of class, students were asked to write what they learned that period. Some teachers balked at journaling, due to the additional work required to periodically read the journals. Other teachers made good use of teacher aides to read journals and look for the concepts the students were expected to learn.

Somewhat contrary to my philosophy on conceptual learning is my approach to learning multiplication facts. Mental math techniques work well for addition facts, but multiplication tables need to be memorized. I loved to use a 10x10 one hundred chart. When it came time to memorize their threes, students were to circle the multiples of 3 on the hundreds chart up to 27. Then, using the chart, they would be quizzed on the threes. After several repetitions, they were encouraged to turn the chart face down and they were again tested. The same procedure was used for the rest of the multiplication tables up to nine. I would highly recommend having students state the fact orally before giving the product. I would also suggest having them always say the lesser of the two factors first. For example, for 9x7 the student would say 7x9 = 63. Think about it! Now they only need to memorize about half as many facts. Also, by the time they have memorized through their sixes they only have 7x7, 7x8, 7x9, 8x8, 8x9, and 9x9 left to learn.

> *Tell me and I forget. Teach me and I*
> *remember. Involve me and I learn.*
> —Ben Franklin

CLASSROOM MANAGEMENT STRATEGIES

Most, if not all, students prefer a structured classroom. At Calvin Coolidge, our school mission statement emphasized the importance of providing a school environment that was both physically and psychologically safe. It was difficult for me not to intercede, at times, when I was in the process of observing teachers in their classrooms. It was particularly unnerving when a teacher would try to talk over their class. One student commented, "If the teacher's yelling, I know everything's okay. When she stops, I know it's time to listen!" Another student stated, "If it's important, she is sure to repeat it!"

As a teacher with a new class of students, I found it very helpful from the very first day to be able to call every student by name. When I had a particularly disruptive student, I found that simply taking a student aside and quietly asking for their cooperation always helped.

In my first year of teaching high school, I was warned by several other teachers that I was sure to be challenged by Sam. I found it was not because Sam was a weak student. On the contrary, Sam was very bright! I quickly made Sam one of my classroom assistants. Whenever I was busy helping one student, they could go to him for help. Sam actually made my job easier.

Then there was another time when two boys began a scuffle in the middle of a testing situation. I had no choice but to send them to the office for fighting. After the class period, I went to the dean to see what I could do to keep them from suspensions. He said if I wrote the referral as a "skirmish" and not a fight he would just keep them in the office for the rest of the day. Years later, these two boys were still my good, close friends.

A few years later as a middle school principal, I was fortunate to have teachers on my staff who were student-centered. Often when they had no choice but to send a student to the office, they would follow their referral with a plea for no suspension. Some teachers would want troublesome students suspended just so they did not have to deal with them. These caring teachers, however, were willing to be part of a better solution. They, too, made my job a lot easier!

PARENT INVOLVEMENT

Students in my math class were rewarded if they could solve the stumper posted daily on the classroom wall. Collaboration with parents or other students was encouraged. I'll never forget the afternoon when one young student hurried back into my classroom to quickly copy the stumper into her folder before her bus departed. "My parents told me never to come home without the stumper," she said, because they routinely discussed it around the dinner table.

On another occasion, a parent revealed to me how shocked he was when he asked his son what he learned in school that day only to have him say, "I'll show you!" The boy then took a paper and pencil, drew a cell, then labeled and explained the internal parts. The father said he expected the usual reply, "Nothing much!"

This is the type of story I like to use to show how important it is to involve students in their own education and encourage more communication with their families.

DEALING WITH COLLEAGUES AND STRUGGLING STUDENTS

Some of the more uncomfortable moments during my time teaching high school involved occasional ill will from my colleagues. After my first semester, I was teaching more of the high-level math classes. This did not always sit well with a couple of teachers, as I was a new teacher being assigned the best classes. I'm sure my good fortune resulted from parents advocating for their kids. On one occasion, I had to confide in a fellow teacher that his son was cheating on my algebra tests. This was initially met with some resistance! I offered after school help and pleaded with my colleague for his son's attendance. After the student participated, there was no more need for him to bend the rules.

At Woodruff High School, we had several students struggling with math. I offered an after school tutoring session and encouraged these students to attend. Those who attended frequently ended up being some of my top math students. During one of my after school tutoring sessions, I was surprised to see another of my math teacher friends observing in the back of my classroom. He said his students were questioning him about why he was not offering after school help like Mr. Millen.

I recall another somewhat humorous tale involving student cheating, which occurred as I wondered if I was putting too much emphasis on homework. As I was checking off students' papers, I couldn't help but notice one boy's work was a Xerox copy of a classmate's work. Upon confronting him, I played dumb and acted as if I was not sure which assignment was a copy and which was the original. Guess what? The young man started doing his own homework and refrained from using the copy machine in his father's office—at least for his algebra assignments!

ONE SEMESTER WAS ENOUGH

One of the most challenging assignments in my educational tenure occurred in the spring of 1993, when I spent a semester as an Interim Director of Middle Schools for Peoria Public Schools. It was challenging because of the decisions necessary regarding student discipline and staff situations across the district. During my first week, I was called to two middle schools: One where the principal was dealing with an irate parent, and a second situation where a teacher was being unprofessional. This was not my idea of using positivity.

Along with assisting principals, this job required reading and approving suspension write-ups that had come in the previous day. It was depressing and demoralizing to encounter so many negative situations. One referral stands out in my memory, however, as it made me laugh out loud. One of the heftier principals sent in the following write-up: "Jimmy was sent to my office today for using a swear word in the classroom. After listening to his side of the story, I was inclined to give him some slack. That was until Jimmy called me a 'fat ass'. That was when I decided a suspension was in order."

I'M LOW TECH

It was difficult for my close friends to believe that I (Mr. Millen) incorporated some of the first personal computers into my teaching for Peoria Public Schools. Back in the 1970s, I acquired two TRS-80 Radio Shack computers to use with my math classes. A converted closet became my first computer lab. Students wrote computer programs for algorithms, such as amortization tables, and then had to save them on cassette tapes.

Not long after that, word got out that computers were in use in one of the district's middle schools. Parents of some high school students complained to the superintendent that this was unfair because there were no computers in the high schools. My principal, John Garrett, was told by the Superintendent of Peoria Public Schools that we needed to remove our computers. Principal Garrett replied, "Why don't you just tell the high schools to buy some?" I got to keep my TRS-80s, and my students continued their programming.

A couple of years later, I was part of a committee that voted to purchase more sophisticated IBM personal computers. I was now provided an additional classroom for my ten new computers. This room became my very popular "computer lab."

After we brought computer technology into the Peoria middle schools, a colleague and I were asked to write a computer literacy curriculum. As a result, we provided a curriculum guide along with picture slides to support the teachers. It was fascinating to reveal that the first calculator (the ENIAC) was about the size of a gymnasium. Its vacuum tubes often needed replacement several times each day.

During my first year using the IBM computers, I found myself toting a central processing unit (CPU) and a large TV type monitor to my home every weekend so I could write programs to use with my students the following week. I benefited from having the one computer lab in our school. If a student received a top test score on a math exam, they received a free pass to the computer lab. One of my students opted not to cash in his free passes but instead proudly decorated his math folder with the certificates he earned.

The 1994 school year was the beginning of my evolution (or devolution) as a high-tech dropout. As a newly appointed middle school principal, I was overwhelmed by the demands of technology in developing schedules and completing reports. I saw several of my principal friends nearly landlocked in their offices due to their attention to technology demands.

I decided that I could not be the leader I wanted to be if I was required to live in my office staring at a computer screen. I soon found a secretary with excellent computer skills who was also anxious to relocate to my school. After a long fight, I won her services! Not only did she take care of my technology needs, but she also served as a resource for many other secretaries across the school district.

I consider this hire to be one of the most significant personnel moves of my career. Freeing myself from the demands of technology allowed me time to work in the classrooms, monitor the hallways and develop successful programs. Had I not made this move, I would have missed out on many of the stories I'm sharing in this book. My granddaughter, however, still reminds me that I'm not very "high tech". I've yet to respond by calling her a snob!

ACADEMIC SUCCESS

O ver the years, I have had the privilege of tutoring many students in general math, algebra and geometry. I became more and more aware that "math anxiety" is rampant in our world. I often heard parents say they understood why their child struggled with math since they were not good at it either. This is a common myth, and it is wrong! I have never worked with a student who did not have the potential to excel at math, but many of them suffered from a severe lack of confidence.

Math proficiency is so important in our lives. It enhances our self-esteem. It often determines a student's course of study. Too often, students will fail to pursue their preferred interests just to avoid the required math courses. I would also argue that many discipline problems start with academic failure. None of us would enjoy going to work each day only to be reminded of our shortcomings.

Whether you think you can or think you can't, you're right!
—Henry Ford

LESSONS FOR MATH EMPOWERMENT

The following chapter provides a sampling of the strategies, topics and lessons I have used to empower students. These lessons enable the learner to see meaningful connections that often lead to long-term retention of some fundamental mathematical concepts. Then, as students become more enlightened in their mathematical competence and problem-solving skills, more doors to their future studies will open for them. There is a high correlation between math requirements and logical reasoning and one's ability to apply tenacity to everyday challenges.

Place Value

A very important but often misunderstood mathematical concept in our Hindu Arabic number system is that of place value. One of my favorite stories relates how one student was inspired when exposed to this concept.

Years ago, a colleague adopted a young girl who had been living in a Russian orphanage. Her new mother related stories of how Sarah adapted to her new life in America. On one occasion she gave Sarah an apple for a snack and was shocked when she watched her eat the entire apple, seeds, stem and all. In the orphanage, one learned not to waste a bit of food! Now it became my charge to catch Sarah up to third grade math.

Initially, Sarah put up some resistance to my approaches. On our third meeting, I asked Sarah to help make a place value chart. We used a penny for the hundredths column, a dime for the tenths column and monopoly money above the ones, tens and hundreds column. We had to design a thousand-dollar bill.

I wasn't sure how much progress I had made with this visual approach until a couple days later when I received a call from Sarah's mother. She was excited to tell me how Sarah had come home from our tutoring session, made her own place value chart, took it to school and taught it to her classmates the next day! Wow!

Make a Simpler Problem (Empowering)

On a following page, you'll find a worksheet called solving problems (using a simpler example). If a student was unsure how to find the missing divisor in a given equation, they could use a simple model. In the given worksheet, looking at the problem $169 \div c = 13$, the student might, for example, write $12 \div \mathbf{3} = 4$, since $12 \div 4 = 3$. Then it would be easy for the student to see that the missing dividend can be found by dividing 169 by 13. Now that they have done the thinking, a powerful tool (the calculator) is left to do the work!

For each problem on the following worksheet, the student is instructed to write a simple fact for that particular operation and then solve the problem.

Solving Problems
(Using a Simpler Example)

Problem: 428 + ☐ = 959
Example:
Solution:

Problem: 43 * ☐ = 8643
Example:
Solution:

Problem: ☐ * 15 = 345
Example:
Solution:

Problem: 2437 – ☐ = 888
Example:
Solution:

Problem: ☐ – 237 = 599
Example:
Solution:

Problem: ☐ ÷ 16 = 244
Example:
Solution:

Problem: 169 ÷ ☐ = 13
Example:
Solution:

Problem: 5555 – ☐ = 4321
Example:
Solution:

Problem: 423 + ☐ = 888
Example:
Solution:

Problem: 4237 ÷ ☐ = 223
Example:
Solution:

The Metric System

The metric system correlates well with our base ten number system. I delivered model lessons for math classes in several middle schools in Peoria. I even went so far as to record a video of my presentation. Then I was able to share this empowering topic with more teachers and their students. I always tried to learn from these teaching experiences and make every lesson more meaningful. If I asked a class to estimate the number of meters it was from the floor to the ceiling, I would get some wild answers! That was until I gave them a frame of reference. I used a golf club as a model of about one meter. My students were even more surprised to learn they had a built-in ruler when I asked them to measure the length of their textbook by using the width of their pinky finger as an approximate centimeter.

As an example of how effective modeling can be, I want to recount a time years later when a young lady approached me at a school athletic event. She said, "Didn't you come to my school and teach us metrics?" In response, I asked, "If I did, how long is a centimeter?" she promptly put up her finger—her pinky finger, of course!

On another occasion, one of my students needed to prepare for a test on metric conversions. Converting within the metric system should be much easier than converting in our English system where you have to remember facts like one mile equals 5,280 feet! In our lesson we drew some stairsteps and labeled each step going up from milli to kilo. To convert 2.6 kilograms to centigrams, one would simply move the decimal point five places to the right down the stairsteps. Thus, 2.6 kilograms equals 260,000 centigrams!

The sad conclusion to this story, however, happened when my student was taking his test. When his teacher saw him drawing this metric stairstep model he stopped him, assuming this had to be cheating. To the contrary, these were exactly the modeling tools we should be using to empower all students!

Pattern Blocks

A popular and commonly used set of manipulatives are called "pattern blocks". I'm enclosing a picture of the four pattern shapes I use to help students better understand fraction equivalents and operations involving fractions and mixed numbers.

The hexagon block will represent one unit. During the initial activity students find as many ways as they can to build a hexagon using trapezoids, rhombuses and equilateral triangles. Following this, they show equivalents (one trapezoid equals three triangles).

The next challenge would be to ask students if they can show how to add or subtract operations with fractions and mixed numbers using pattern blocks only. Using these shapes for showing how to complete the operation 2 1/3 − 1 1/2 = □ would require equivalent exchanges and regrouping.

I like incorporating geometry terms and figures into the development of fraction concepts. Students have been heard to remark, "I didn't know you could see fractions!"

Sample of pattern block manipulatives

Making Connections with Money

One of the most effective ways for teachers to empower their students to be good problem solvers is by showing them how to make real life connections. I'm including a model of how teachers can use money to help students better understand fraction, decimal and percentage concepts.

Students are provided a sheet of rectangles that are divided into halves, fourth, fifths and tenths. Assuming each rectangle represents one dollar, they are instructed to show an equal distribution of 100 cents within each sector. Then to the left of each rectangle they list four ways to name an indicated amount. Completing a model for 1/2, 1/4, 3/4, 1/5, 2/5, 3/5, 4/5, 1/10, 3/10, 7/10 and 9/10 will help them make connections and strengthen these concepts.

MONEY CONNECTIONS

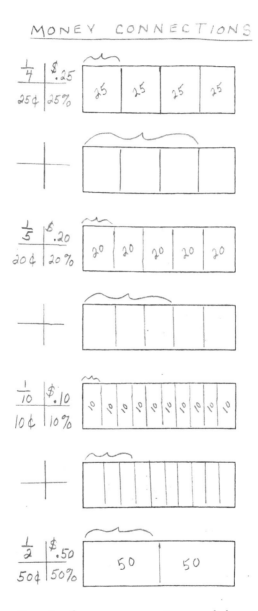

Sample of money connections worksheet

Understanding Quantities

We use, read, hear and see quantities expressed in the amounts of hundreds, thousands, millions, billions and even trillions every day. The following activities could help us all better understand the magnitude of these terms.

1. To help his students get a grasp on the concept of a million, a colleague told his class he would give ten dollars to anyone who could write out the numerals from one to one million. One student completed the challenge, but only by having a computer generate the entire sequence. She used a couple dollars' worth of printer paper!

2. Another colleague invested in a box of rubber bands and a few boxes of toothpicks. The round toothpicks came 250 per box. Four boxes bundled made a ring of 1,000. (This already saved some counting.)

    Now if this ring of toothpicks represented the cross-section of a small tree, a thousand sections stacked one on top of another would represent one million toothpicks. Could this tree be many stories tall? To build 1,000 trees would require a billion toothpicks. Please save your money on purchases of toothpicks and rubber bands.

3. Wait! If the United States Government can spend trillions of dollars, let's at least try to understand

the enormousness of a trillion. Counting dollar bills one at a time, let's assume it would take a minute to count out each hundred, then one thousand in ten minutes, and one million in ten thousand minutes. (Are you getting tired yet?)

At this stage, it would be enlightening to convert ten thousand minutes to hours 10,000 ÷ 60 = 166 2/3 hours or about a week. If one wants to keep going, it would take one thousand weeks or over nineteen years to count out one billion dollars. (No time off for eating or sleeping!) Now, since a trillion is one thousand billion, in 19,000 years one will have counted out enough money for Congress to spend another one trillion dollars! How many lifetimes could this be?

4. A suggested math class assignment: Challenge students to see who can come up with the most interesting way to understand the concepts of millions, billions and trillions.

Scrabble Math

This activity involves determining the frequency of each letter of the alphabet occurring in everyday text. Each student in the class is assigned a paragraph in a book selected at random. They then count how often they find each letter—A to Z—in their paragraph. On the following page is a bar graph example of one student's results.

The students are then instructed to combine their results into a master graph. Handheld calculators become powerful tools as they enable the students to total large sums and then determine percentages of each letter's occurrence. The most meaningful aspect happens when the students are asked to brainstorm how this information could be used. Following are a few possibilities:

1. If we repeat this activity could we expect the same or similar results?

2. How closely did individual student graphs compare to the class master?

3. Would Wheel of Fortune contestants find this information helpful when making their letter selections?

4. Each student would be encouraged to write a message in their own made-up codes. They then exchange their coded message with a classmate and are encouraged to use their frequency graphs to help break the codes.

Scrabble Math can help students develop an appreciation for statistics. College programs often require a class in statistics. This activity also puts emphasis on the proper use of technology. Calculators are put in the students' hands at the appropriate time. They do the research and then the calculators are the tools that do the work.

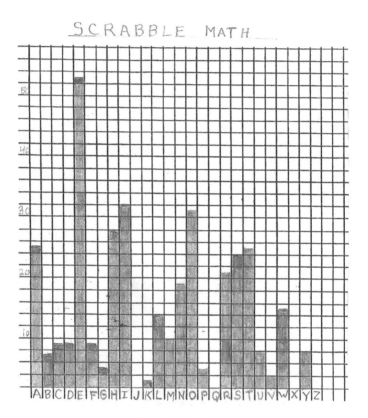

Sample of Scrabble Graph

Math Tricks

When I was teaching, it was not unusual to be asked to cover for another teacher's class. Sometimes this would be spur of the moment and I would pull out one of my math tricks to keep the students occupied.

I choose not to conclude my book by releasing all my secrets but will share one of my favorites here! I'll save the rest for my next book.

Step #1: Ask the students to each write down a three-digit number using three different digits, like 472.

Step #2: Have them each write a six-digit number by repeating the same three digits. Using the example in Step #1, this would be 472,472.

Step #3: Have them divide their six-digit number by the lucky number seven. Then ask how many had a whole number quotient. All should have!

Step #4: Have them divide their new quotient by the unlucky number 13. Again, they will get a whole number result. (You can redo the computation for any doubters.)

Step #5: Say, "Just for fun, let's divide your last quotient by 11."

Step #6: Ask the students to share their results. The quotient will be their original three-digit number.

This "trick" is based on a good mathematical principle called the fundamental theorem of arithmetic. Every integer greater than 1 can be written as a product of primes. 7 x 11 x 13 = 1001

1001 x 472 = 472,472

I hope you enjoy using the ideas, activities and stories I've shared in this book!

ABOUT THE AUTHOR

The awards, honors and recognitions bestowed upon Gary Millen throughout his sixty plus years as a mentor, teacher, coach, principal and mathematics consultant give tremendous credibility to the philosophy of positivity and proactivity promoted throughout this book. After his initial five years in a Title 1 junior high school, Gary was recruited to teach mathematics in Peoria Public Schools' gifted program. At Washington School, teachers were expected to go above and beyond to meet and exceed the needs of their students, and Gary met that challenge head on. His first award came in 1975 from the Peoria Jaycees when he received their outstanding Young Educators Award. This was followed by the Mary Kooyumjian Award as one of the three top gifted teachers in the State of Illinois. This award came from the Illinois Council for the Gifted.

In 1984, the Illinois State Board of Education named Mr. Millen as one of Illinois Master Teachers. As a result of this honor, he was granted released time from his teaching responsibilities, which enabled him to make numerous presentations locally and statewide on mathematics strategies. As a teacher and coach, Gary took several teams of students to the Illinois State Mathcounts competition held at Millikin University in Decatur, Illinois.

In 1991, the Peoria Board of Education elevated Mr. Millen to the position of mathematics staff developer. His job duties required close consultation with all the district's grade 5-12 math teachers. Expectations included improving instruction, developing lessons and conducting model teaching demonstrations. After two years in the position, the Peoria School Board named Mr. Millen "Educator of the Year" presenting him with the Don Phares Excellence in Education Award. This award is the highest honor the district bestows on an educator in Peoria Public Schools.

In 1994, Gary was promoted to the principalship of Calvin Coolidge Middle School in West Peoria. During the next seven years, numerous District 150 personnel and Calvin Coolidge staff received distinguished awards as a result of Mr. Millen's nominations. These individuals included teachers as well as a secretary, a parent, a coach, a security guard, a library manager, a bus driver and a transportation supervisor.

In 1999, as a school administrator, Gary received the Award of Excellence from the Illinois State Board of Education and was honored at their annual awards banquet in Springfield, Illinois.

Prior to retiring in 2001, Mr. Millen received two more honors. They were the Lifetime Distinguished Service Award from the Jaycees and the Bill Houlihan Champions for Children Advocacy Award. The latter was presented during the Children's Miracle Network Champions broadcast on WEEK-TV25 in 2001.

After his retirement in the spring of 2001, Gary continued to promote mathematics teaching as he was recruited by Peoria area administrators to serve as a math consultant for K-8 teachers.

Those Who Excel Billboard

This billboard towered over several businesses on Western Avenue in Peoria, Illinois. The picture shows Mr. Millen after receiving the distinguished "Those Who Excel" education award from the Illinois State Board of Education.

CPSIA information can be obtained
at www.ICGtesting.com
Printed in the USA
LVHW111528040821
694535LV00004B/355

9 780228 848301